The Tudor Rose Maze fills the main courtyard at Kentwell Hall, an Elizabethan manor house in Suffolk.

MAZES

Adrian Fisher
and
Diana Kingham

Shire Publications Ltd

CONTENTS

Published in 1997 by Shire Publications Ltd, Cromwell House, Church Street, Princes Risborough, Buckinghamshire HP27 9AA, UK.

Printed in Great Britain by CIT Printing Services, Press Buildings, Merlins Bridge, Haverfordwest, Pembrokeshire SA61 1XF.

British Library Cataloguing in Publication Data: Fisher, Adrian. Mazes. 1. Mazes. I. Title. II. Kingham, Diana. 717. ISBN 0-7478-0116-9.

ACKNOWLEDGEMENTS
Illustrations are acknowledged as follows: Adrian Fisher, cover and pages 1, 2, 3, 4, 5, 7, 8 (top left and bottom), 10 (bottom), 16, 17, 19 and 21-9; George Gerster, page 19; Hampton Court Palace, page 13; Diana Kingham, page 11; National Museum of Wales, page 7 (bottom); Jeff Saward, pages 8 (top right) and 9; Bo Stjernstrom, page 6; Lord Somerleyton, page 15.

Cover: *Hever Castle maze in Kent, viewed from the castle battlements. It epitomises the well-maintained puzzle hedge maze.*

Below: *The site of Joseph Paxton's famous glasshouse at Chatsworth, Derbyshire, is now occupied by a hedge maze. Although the maze was planted only in 1962, it is beautifully in keeping with the surrounding historic garden. It is not open to the public but can be viewed from outside.*

The Archbishop's Maze at Greys Court in Oxfordshire was dedicated by Dr Robert Runcie, Archbishop of Canterbury, in 1981. It is a modern interpretation of a Christian turf maze and abounds in Christian symbolism. The brick paths are set in a circular arrangement between turf barriers.

WHAT IS A MAZE?

To most of us the word 'maze' conjures up a picture of a hedge maze, like the one at Hampton Court. The network of paths forms an intricate complex of turns, junctions and dead ends all concealed between rows of tall hedges. Such mazes are designed to confuse and frustrate travellers in their quest to reach the goal. But hedge mazes are just one relatively recent development of a theme which has been explored by mankind for thousands of years. During their long history mazes have been used variously as a means of warding off evil, a method of ensuring fertility, a form of Christian devotion and a focus of village festivities.

Mazes come in a wide variety of shapes and sizes. They do not conform to a simple definition but they do possess certain distinctive characteristics. They contain twists and turns, have a deliberate and pleasing design, are man-made and promote movement along their course towards the goal.

In English the two words 'maze' and 'labyrinth' are generally synonymous.

There are two basic types of maze. All the early mazes are of the *unicursal*, or single-pathed, design with just one path leading from the outside to the centre. There are no junctions or decision points, and every part of the path is walked once and once only. Traditional turf mazes and stone labyrinths are unicursal. The other main type, of which the puzzle hedge maze is an example, is a later invention probably dating from the seventeenth century. This is the more familiar *multicursal* design, which has a series of dead ends leading off the one true path, providing scope for puzzlement and confusion.

What is it that makes the maze so enduring and fascinating a device? Over thousands of years and in the mythologies of diverse cultures the maze has been consistently associated with courtship and fertility, death and rebirth. Its convoluted paths

Left: *Thomas Hill's unicursal design for a low-growing maze planted with evergreens was designed to be viewed from an upstairs window or as a walk rather than as a puzzle. (From 'The Profitable Art of Gardening', 1568.)*

Right: *The plan of the Hampton Court Maze shows it to be multicursal, with junctions and dead-end paths leading off the one true path. All hedges are joined to the perimeter hedge, which makes the maze relatively simple to solve.*

Below: *The goal of the world famous Hampton Court Maze may seem surprisingly small. The overhanging trees add to the feeling of a secret and special place that cannot easily be found.*

offer protection by denying access to the uninitiated; labyrinths were chalked on doorway thresholds to keep out evil spirits. The pagan labyrinth was adopted and adapted by the Christian church and later by garden designers.

Even today, mystery, confusion and symbolism continue to be firmly associated with the maze. The words 'maze' and 'labyrinth' are used as metaphors for bewilderment and complexity. Mazes continue to stimulate concentration, awareness and a determination to reach the goal in those who enter them. Once inside, people experience various emotions ranging from unease, frustration, claustrophobia and contemplation to the sense of liberation shown by children who are moved to run and shout for joy when they enter a maze.

EARLY ORIGINS AND MYTHS

Until about AD1000 just one archetypal design of maze prevailed throughout the world. This was the Classical (sometimes known as Cretan) type of labyrinth. The design, which comprises seven rings of paths contained within eight concentric rings of barriers, is easy to draw. It has been carved on rocks, chalked on thresholds and copied as full-sized turf mazes and stone labyrinths for many hundreds of years and throughout the world.

The origins of the maze are lost in history. Its precursors were the cup and ring marks and spiral designs drawn and carved by early man, which hint at a preoccupation with the inner spirit and the journey through life to death. The labyrinth probably evolved from the spiral design when man started devising geometric constructions.

It is possible that the Classical labyrinth evolved more than once in different parts of the world independently. Once learnt, the design is easy to construct from a central cross and four dots, and it is easy to memorise and pass on; the design may have an inherent mathematical fascination. Whilst the design may not have changed, the cultural significance of the maze may have become lost or confused before being adopted by another culture and given a new meaning.

Several cultures have produced their own labyrinth myths. The best known is the Greek legend of Theseus and the Minotaur. The Minotaur, half man and half bull, was imprisoned in a labyrinth designed by Daedalus for King Minos of Crete. As a result of losing a war to Crete, every nine years Athens was obliged to send seven young men and seven maidens to be sacrificed to the Minotaur. Theseus, son of the king of Athens, went as one of the group, determined to kill the Minotaur and end the tribute. He persuaded King Minos's daughter Ariadne to provide him with a golden thread with which he marked his path through the labyrinth; he reached the centre, slew the Minotaur and escaped with his companions and Ariadne from Crete.

The Classical labyrinth was illustrated on the reverse of Cretan coinage, representing the one made by Daedalus, but the structure must have been much more complicated, if it existed. No evidence of a labyrinth was found in excavations of King Minos' palace. The name 'labyrinth' is thought to derive from the Greek *labrys*, the ritual double-headed axe of the Minoan civilisation on Crete, which formed part of the cult of the bull.

In the mythology of the Tohono O'otam and Pima tribes of southern Arizona in the United States, the Classical labyrinth represents the home of Iitoi. Iitoi resembles a combination of the characters of Noah and Christ in the Old and New Testaments. The maze, which represents his mysterious and bewildering journey from the tribal villages to his mountain home, is used to distance him from his followers. Entry into the labyrinth gives Iitoi new life, so that he achieves reincarnation and immortality. The labyrinth symbolises individual, family and tribal rebirth; Iitoi's path through it is his path through life as he acquires knowledge and understanding. The centre represents death, which he transcends.

Diagram showing the construction of the seven-ringed 'Classical' or 'Cretan' type of maze design. It is thought that the reason for the long and widespread popularity of the Classical design lies in the simple method of drawing it from a cross and four dots.

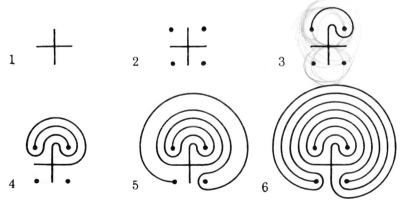

A stone labyrinth of Classical design with rows of boulders to form barriers between the paths. Mazes of this kind are found extensively along the Scandinavian coast.

ANCIENT AND MEDIEVAL MAZES

The oldest labyrinths are of the Classical design and are carved on rocks; probably the earliest, in Sardinia, was inscribed in about 1600 BC. The dating of isolated rock carvings is difficult, as proved to be the case with three similar designs from the British Isles carved on rocks. The Hollywood Stone, displayed in the National Museum, Dublin, was originally thought to be neolithic (1800-1400 BC) but is now dated to about AD 550. Two labyrinths found carved on the rock wall of the Rocky Valley, near Tintagel, Cornwall, were thought to be bronze age (about 2000 BC) but may have been carved as recently as the late seventeenth century by a reputedly brilliant though illiterate mathematician who owned the adjacent mill.

ROMAN MOSAIC MAZES

The Romans adopted the Classical labyrinth design and adapted it to a more complex form in their mosaic pavements. Some fifty examples have been found throughout the Roman Empire, spanning a period from about 100 BC to AD 400. The most typical design consists of four meanders which are linked but which effectively divide the square area into four regular sections; the path must be followed methodically, proceeding quarter by quarter. Many of these mosaic labyrinths are representations of a fortified city, possibly Troy, with a turreted perimeter, four arterial roads and a tortuous street pattern. Very few of these mosaics are large enough to allow the paths to be walked on and so must have been designed to be purely contemplative and decorative.

The Minoan legend is often represented in Roman labyrinths. In some mosaics scenes of the legend are depicted in the centre, the most common being Theseus slaying the Minotaur. In Pompeii a square form of the Classical design was found scratched on a painted pillar with the inscription *Labyrinthus hic habit Minotaurus* around it.

Six Roman labyrinth mosaics have been found in Britain including an 11 feet (3.35 metres) square complete pavement mosaic found at Harpham, Humberside, formerly displayed in the City Hall at Hull, and a damaged pavement mosaic from Caerleon, Gwent, now in the Roman Legionary Museum at Caerleon.

STONE LABYRINTHS

In Scandinavia over five hundred full-sized stone labyrinths of the Classical design have been recorded, mainly along the Baltic coast. These labyrinths are constructed by laying rows of boulders to form the barriers between the paths. Some are associated with prehistoric burials and may date back as far as the bronze age, but most are medieval or later. Until the early twentieth century fishermen walked the paths of the labyrinths before putting to sea to ensure good catches and favourable winds and to protect themselves from evil spirits. Some labyrinths have names such as Troy, Jericho or Jerusalem which suggest that these labyrinths represented a walled city or fortification which only the initiated could enter. Some labyrinths were used in courtship dances by young people, unknown to their parents and elders. In some a virgin stood at the centre while others danced in procession towards her. In others a boy would run the paths to reach the girl or win her as part of the universal mating ritual.

Few stone labyrinths occur in Britain, and all but one are the result of a resurgence of interest in modern times. The exception is on St Agnes in the Scilly Isles and is reputed to have been built in 1726 by a lighthouse keeper. There is no record of why he made it.

THE MEDIEVAL CHRISTIAN MAZE

The pagan labyrinth was adopted by the medieval Christian church and adapted for its own use by including Christian symbolism in the design. The earliest surviving full-sized example is the 'Chemin de Jerusalem' pavement maze in the nave of Chartres Cathedral, France, built in 1235. Such mazes became a feature of Gothic churches in northern France. They represented the path of life and reflected the recent journeys of the Crusaders; reaching the centre symbolised reaching both Jerusalem and salvation. They were designed as a penitential circuit to be completed upon the knees to gain forgiveness of sins, or to be walked as a substitute for a pilgrimage to the Holy Land.

The medieval Christian maze was characteristically cruciform in design, with eleven

A carving of a Classical labyrinth on the wall of the Rocky Valley, Cornwall. This is the predominant design of ancient labyrinths and is found repeatedly throughout Europe and North America.

The incomplete Roman mosaic pavement discovered in the churchyard at Caerleon, Gwent, is thought to date from the second or third century AD. Most Roman mosaic labyrinths are square in form, possibly because they are easier to lay than round versions.

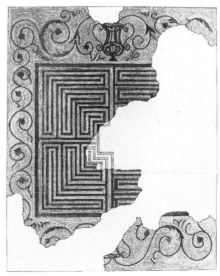

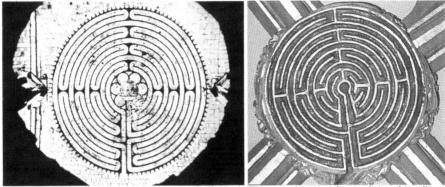

Left: *The pavement maze in Chartres Cathedral, France, showing the traditional medieval Christian design with its emphasised central cruciform motif. These pavement mazes were not built in English churches, but the design is very similar to many British turf mazes.*

Right: *A fifteenth-century maze, just 8 inches (20 cm) across, carved on the roof boss in St Mary Redcliffe church in Bristol, Avon. The eleven-ringed medieval Christian design is painted in black and gold.*

rings of paths (rather than the seven of the Classical labyrinth), and, most significantly, the paths ranged freely through the quadrants rather than proceeding methodically through each quarter in the Roman way. There were two main forms of the design, with either circular paths (as at Chartres) or octagonal ones. Pavement mazes were not found in English churches of this period, but the design is found in other types of mazes dating from the medieval period or later.

EARLY TURF MAZES

Turf mazes, like stone labyrinths, are an ancient form of maze, although their precise origin, purpose and subsequent usage are uncertain. They are found mainly in central and southern Britain, although there are a few examples in Germany and Poland. Possibly turf mazes were the southern counterpart of the stone labyrinth, cut at sites where boulders were not readily available, and they may be of great antiquity. Precise dating is not possible without the

The turf maze at Hilton, Cambridgeshire, located in a corner of the green. The maze is 55 feet (17 metres) in diameter and is a nine-ring medieval Christian design; records show it was formerly eleven-ringed. The present maze has been recut wrongly near the middle at some time.

support of written records.

Typically, the paths were of turf with gulleys cut into the turf as barriers, in some areas exposing the white chalk beneath. Occasionally this arrangement was reversed so that the paths lay in the gulleys and strips of turf formed the barriers. Only eight of the sixty known sites in Britain have survived but once there may have been more than one hundred.

Turf mazes were designed to be walked or run along, following the path from the outside along its tortuous route to the cen-tre, a feat which demands intense concentration. They were usually found on village greens and were probably used for maze running on festive occasions such as Easter and May Day to celebrate renewed fertility after the winter. Turf mazes may also have been used for maypole dancing and other May Day ceremonies, as well as providing additional attractions for festivals and fairs. They were also associated with courtship dances similar to those danced in Scandinavian stone labyrinths.

There are two types of British turf maze,

Plans of four lost turf mazes. (Left, above) Robin Hood's Race at Sneinton, Nottinghamshire. (Left, below) Walls of Troy in Holderness, Humberside, was an unusually shaped maze some 40 feet (12 metres) in diameter. It was destroyed after 1815. (Right, above) Pimperne, Dorset, had the largest recorded turf maze, with a unique meandering design. (Right, below) The Shepherd's Race at Broughton Green, Northamptonshire, was destroyed by the Army in the First World War.

A fanciful view, popularised by the Victorians, of monks traversing the turf maze at Sneinton, Nottinghamshire, on their knees as a form of religious penance.

defined by their design and inspiration. The oldest type was cut in the Classical design and the mazes were called by such names as Troy Town, Julian's Bower and Maiden's Bower, identical to those of the Scandinavian stone labyrinths. Only two such mazes now remain, one in a private garden at Somerton, Oxfordshire, and the other at Dalby, North Yorkshire. The latter is Britain's smallest turf maze, 26 by 20 feet (8 by 6.1 metres), recut on its present site in the 1890s as a copy of a much older maze.

The later type of English turf maze is of medieval Christian design. The continuity of pagan names for many of these mazes suggests that the medieval Christian design may have replaced an earlier Classical turf maze on the same site. It is probable that the Christian church, faced with a deeply rooted tradition of pagan turf mazes, simply replaced them with their own more acceptable form and allowed their use to continue with the blessing of the church. Other turf mazes may be post-medieval in origin and would always have been of this later design.

A turf maze needs constant maintenance and can be lost entirely within a few years. The records of the Saffron Walden maze, Essex, show that recutting was carried out in 1828, 1841, 1859 and 1887. In 1911 bricks were laid in the gulley to form a path which gave the maze greater permanence, and further restoration work was carried out in 1979. The need to recut turf mazes, often following periods of neglect, has led to slight but crucial errors in the design of many of them.

The largest surviving turf maze is at Saffron Walden, Essex; it has raised corner bastions and a central mound. This seventeen-ringed medieval Christian design measures 132 feet (40.6 metres) from corner to corner. A large ash tree is said to have formerly grown in the centre.

A low maze of dwarf box hedging forming part of Lady Salisbury's new knot garden at Hatfield House, Hertfordshire. This style of maze was popular in sixteenth and seventeenth-century gardens.

EARLY GARDEN MAZES

By the fifteenth century, a new type of maze arose which no longer had a ritual or religious significance. Mazes with barriers of vegetation became popular as ornamental features in French and Italian Renaissance gardens. Even earlier, Charles V of France (reigned 1364-80) is recorded as having a labyrinth amongst the features in his pleasure garden at the Hotel St Pol. It is difficult to know when garden mazes first became popular in England, little information being available before detailed pictures of gardens were produced in the early fifteenth century. However, it appears that by 1494 'a knot in a garden, called a mase' was a commonplace feature.

GARDEN LABYRINTHS

Mazes at this time were designed with no obvious intention to confuse; the barriers between the paths were low and the majority were unicursal in design. Like knot gardens, also characteristic of this period, mazes were designed to be viewed from an upstairs window and to provide year-round interest in the garden.

The plants chosen for mazes and knots were evergreens, including herbs such as thyme, winter savory, hyssop, lavender and marjoram. Intricate designs could be quickly produced with herbs and their scent made the garden delightful to walk through. However, they required frequent trimming to maintain a crisp effect and were short-lived. A more permanent choice for gardens in the early seventeenth century was dwarf box, slow-growing but long-lived, in time growing into a thick low hedge.

Thomas Hill, in his horticultural treatise of 1568 and later works, published two figures of mazes. He recommended them as proper adornments for larger gardens, where they would provide recreation and decoration.

Box could be used on its own to produce low hedge mazes, allowing a quite intricate design to be fitted into a small area. A modern example of this type of maze has been designed by Lady Salisbury at Hatfield House, Hertfordshire, as part of the knot

Above: *A circular design for a labyrinth from Thomas Hill's 'Treatise', which could be used for a low box-hedged maze or set out as a floral labyrinth. Hill suggests planting fruit trees or 'Herbers decked with roses' in the corners and centre.*

Below: *A design for a unicursal floral labyrinth by Vredeman de Vries (1583). It was intended to form part of a formal garden which could be walked through or viewed from above.*

garden in front of the Old Palace. This garden can be viewed from the surrounding raised walkway.

The other kind of low-growing maze was the floral labyrinth, well illustrated by Vredeman de Vries in his *Hortorum Viridariorumque Formae* of 1583. Here the barriers were flower-beds, often edged with dwarf box or clipped herbs, with flowering plants or shrubs growing in the centre. These were much larger mazes, forming distinct areas within the enclosed formal gardens of the period. Floral labyrinths planted with tall shrubs may have been precursors of the hedge maze proper.

EARLY HEDGE MAZES

Towards the end of the sixteenth century mazes were planted with barriers of tall hedges. One early record describes the maze at Nonsuch Palace, Surrey, in 1599 as 'being set round with high plants so that one could neither go over nor through them', obviously a noteworthy feature at this time. These early hedge mazes were probably unicursal in design, as is shown by a sur-

Left: *The Hampton Court Maze is still a popular amusement three hundred years after its planting. Today it has an estimated third of a million visitors annually.*

Below: *A plan of the tall hedge maze at Theobalds, Hertfordshire, shows that it was unicursal in design rather than a puzzle maze. The maze was destroyed during the Civil War.*

viving plan of Lord Burghley's maze at Theobalds in Hertfordshire.

William Lawson in his *A New Orchard and Garden*, written in 1618, includes a maze in his list of desirable garden features. He advocates that it should be made of fruiting shrubs and trees 'well framed a man's height so as to make your friend wander in gathering of berries till he cannot recover himself without your help'. By 1634 the new garden of Prince William of Orange in Holland had, according to Sir William Brereton, 'a remarkable garden in the shape of a square with high, trimmed hedges forming a maze'. The hedges, trained on to wooden supports, were a mixture of evergreen and deciduous shrubs and fruit trees.

The puzzle hedge maze appears to have been the result of Dutch influence, reaching England later in the seventeenth century. The best known British example is the maze at Hampton Court, near London, part of the formal gardens designed by George London and Henry Wise. Records show that the maze was created as part of the final stage of William and Mary's remodelling of the gardens carried out between 1689 and 1696. Its distinctive trapezoid shape was dictated by the intersecting paths of the wilderness area. Originally the maze was planted entirely of hornbeam, but subsequent renewal has resulted in the present patchwork of

species, now predominantly yew.

A further type of hedge maze arose in the late seventeenth century, its aim being to provide an entertaining and diversified walk rather than to puzzle visitors. Instead of paths bounded by hedges of a uniform thickness, these new mazes had winding paths which penetrated blocks of shrub or dense thicket. A well known example is the Labyrinth of Versailles, constructed by J. Hardouin-Mansart in the smaller park in Versailles for Louis XIV. Here, as in many other mazes, the uniformity of the walks was relieved with sculptures, fountains and other features. Within the Versailles labyr-

PLAN DV
LABIRINTHE
DE VERSAILLES.

Left: *A plan of the Versailles labyrinth, France, by Perrault (1677) shows it was not a conventional hedge maze but of the 'block' type, with statues placed at intervals. Here couples could find privacy and escape the stiffness of court etiquette.*

inth were 39 groups of hydraulic statuary representing Aesop's *Fables*.

These 'block' mazes were also popular in England. The one at Trinity College, Oxford, illustrated in *Oxonia Depicta*, is little more than a series of open areas linked by paths; it was destroyed in 1813. Others at Belvoir Castle (Leicestershire), Boughton (Northamptonshire), Exton Park (Leicestershire), Badminton (Avon) and Castle Howard (North Yorkshire) are shown in engravings by Kip (1724) and others.

Written records of mazes indicate their popularity during this period. Several in the vicinity of London are recorded by Samuel Pepys, John Evelyn and John Aubrey, some of which may have been of the puzzle hedge type. However, only the Hampton Court maze still exists, having survived the late eighteenth-century fashion for informal landscapes which destroyed so many existing formal gardens and their features.

Below: *The popularity of block mazes is indicated by the great number of published designs, including this in Batty Langley's 'New Principles of Gardening', 1728.*

14

View of the Somerleyton Maze, Suffolk, with its central mound and pagoda, which form the goal. The maze was planted in 1846 with yew hedges. It measures 245 by 160 feet (75 by 49 metres) and incorporates 440 yards (406 metres) of paths.

THE VICTORIAN REVIVAL

Although the popularity of mazes in private gardens had declined during the late eighteenth century, their popularity in places of public amusement continued. Few records of mazes survive, but they are known to have been attractions at several pleasure gardens in London (Ranelagh Gardens, Vauxhall Gardens, White Conduit House in Islington, and the celebrated Beulah Spa in south London), as well as in the fashionable resorts.

PRIVATE ENTERTAINMENT

By the mid nineteenth century, tastes in private gardens were again swinging back to formality, and hedges, topiary and puzzle hedge mazes once more came into vogue.

An early pioneer of the revival was the fourth Earl Stanhope, who planted a maze at Chevening, Kent, between 1818 and 1830, to a design by the second Earl (1714-86), who was an eminent mathematician. His design was innovative, taking the art of maze design to the most complex two-dimensional form possible. Previously mazes had all their hedges ultimately linked to the perimeter hedge, making their solution relatively simple: by using the 'hand-on-wall' method of consistently turning right (or left) in and out of each dead end, the goal could always be reached. The added complexity was achieved by siting the goal within a separate 'island' of hedges, so that visitors using the 'hand-on-wall' method could not reach the goal and eventually returned to the entrance.

Not all mazes were so formally or regularly designed. A most unusual example can be seen on a sloping hillside at Glendurgan, Cornwall, with waist-high hedges of laurel. The maze was planted in 1833 by Alfred Fox, but there is no evidence of the inspiration behind its conception, execution or meaning.

The 'Italianate' style of gardening became popular during the 1830s and 1840s and sometimes included a maze in the design. The extensive Italian gardens at

Shrublands Hall, Suffolk, created by Sir Charles Barry, included a hedge maze, which has been restored. An Italianate maze has been chosen by Capel Manor, near Enfield, Middlesex, to represent a Victorian garden in its series of garden history reconstructions. The design of the maze was inspired by designs of this period; it was planted with holly in 1989, with a 'secret garden' containing a fountain and statues as its goal.

At Somerleyton Hall in Suffolk William Nesfield designed a yew-hedge maze, planted in 1846, with a delightful central knoll and pagoda. Mazes survive from this period at other houses open to the public, but they are often too small or fragile to withstand many visitors. The notable hedge maze at Hatfield House, Hertfordshire, planted in yew in 1840 and designed by Lord Mahon, is thought to have replaced an earlier maze in the gardens. At Woburn Abbey, Bedfordshire, the small circular maze complete with a central painted pavilion forms part of the private gardens. Neither of these private mazes is open to visitors.

A fine yew-hedge maze was planted by Lord Astor at Hever Castle, Kent, in 1905 as part of his massive restoration programme for the castle and gardens (see cover). The maze formed part of the newly created 'Tudor' garden to the east of the castle, dedicated to Anne Boleyn, whose home the castle was. A maze was included because it was known to be a favourite device of the Tudors although its interpretation as a puzzle hedge maze is inaccurate.

POPULAR LEISURE

Hedge mazes continued to be a popular form of entertainment for the Victorians in many public parks and gardens. William Nesfield was commissioned by Prince Albert to design a maze as part of the Royal Horticultural Society's gardens, now the

Above: *The Italianate Maze at Capel Manor, Middlesex, planted in 1989, recreates the 'Italianate' gardening style popular in England in the 1840s.*

Right: *A plan of the Chevening maze, Kent, showing the innovative use of islands of hedges, one of which contains the goal. This makes the maze far more difficult to solve.*

⬤ PERIMETER HEDGE

⬤ CENTRAL ISLAND

⬤ MINOR ISLANDS

This unusual hedge maze with waist-high laurel hedges is set on the hillside at Glendurgan, Cornwall (National Trust property).

The pavement maze beneath the west tower of Ely Cathedral, Cambridgeshire, was laid in 1870. The maze, of black and white stone, is 20 feet (6.1 metres) square; the total length of the path is 215 feet (66 metres), the height of the tower.

Plan of the Bridge End Gardens Maze, Saffron Walden, Essex, created in 1839 and replanted in 1984 as part of the extensive restoration programme for the gardens.

site of the museums in South Kensington, London, and funded by profits from the 1851 Great Exhibition.

When the Crystal Palace was reopened at Sydenham Hill in 1854, a magnificent park was laid out in Italianate style around it. The maze, not part of the original plan, was built on one of a pair of artificial mounds. Its circles of hornbeam hedges and paths of crushed brick were surrounded by a belt of poplars and rhododendrons. In the central goal were seven trees surrounding a flagpole; a flag with MAZE written on it was hoisted during opening hours. At the entrance was a Swiss-style chalet, where admission tickets costing 3d were sold.

The Crystal Palace maze was one of the well known 'tea-garden' mazes; another was at Rotherville Gardens, Gravesend, Kent. Tea gardens became fashionable as places for Victorian ladies of leisure to visit in the late afternoon around tea time, when strolling in the maze was regarded as an acceptable form of recreation.

Another popular maze was at Bridge End Gardens, Saffron Walden, Essex. It was Italianate in design with semicircular apses and statuary at the goal. The progress of others within the maze could be watched from a central viewing platform, although attempts to work out the plan of the maze from it were thwarted by tall U-shaped topiary arches. Originally designed for his private garden, the maze was rather small for the public use it received when Bridge End Gardens were opened to the populace of Saffron Walden by its owner, Francis

Gibson, in the mid nineteenth century. In 1918 the gardens were leased to the borough but later became neglected and overgrown.

Towards the end of the nineteenth century a number of copies of existing mazes were planted, in both public and private gardens. The most popular was the Hampton Court design, which survives at Tatton Park, Cheshire (1890). Other copies at Albert Park, Middlesbrough, Cleveland (1894), and Knebworth House, Hertfordshire, and an oval version at Mentmore Towers, Buckinghamshire (1899), have since been destroyed. At Castle Bromwich Hall, West Midlands, the now restored maze was found to be a squared mirror image of the Hampton Court Maze, planted in holly and hawthorn during this period. The Chevening design was copied in a Victorian public park in Anerley, Norwood, London, at North Woolwich, London, and at Beauport House near Hastings, East Sussex, all three now lost. In Worden Park, Leyland, Lancashire, a copy of the Somerleyton maze, planted in hornbeam hedging in 1886, remains popular.

CHURCH MAZES

Although pavement mazes were never built in medieval English churches, some were included in Victorian church restoration schemes. The most notable was by Sir Gilbert Scott, built beneath the west tower of Ely Cathedral, Cambridgeshire, in 1870. The maze of black and white stone measuring 20 feet (6.2 metres) square superficially resembles the medieval Christian design found in French cathedrals. In Bourn church, Cambridgeshire, the new floor laid in 1875 included a rectangular copy of the Hampton Court maze in red and black tiles; a font was later placed in the centre of it. Two other Victorian church mazes are at Itchen Stoke in Hampshire and the Watts Memorial Chapel, Compton, Surrey.

The design of the distinctive medieval Christian turf maze at Alkborough, Humberside, was copied in the floor of the porch of the parish church by the lord of the manor, Mr J. G. Constable in 1887, and again in a stained glass window in the church and on his tombstone.

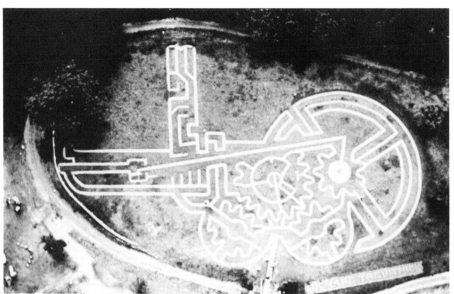

The paths of the Lappa Maze at the Lappa Valley Steam Railway in Cornwall form the shape of Trevithick's steam locomotive. The date of the engine is portrayed in Roman numerals with the design (MDCCCIIII, for 1804).

MODERN MAZES

The social and economic upheaval of two world wars imposed harsh neglect on existing gardens. For half a century it was difficult to maintain gardens, let alone develop them, and many existing mazes were abandoned whilst few new ones were created. Since the 1970s, however, there has been a renaissance in maze building in Britain, and a great number of new mazes have been built. Many of the new generation of mazes are based on elaborate emblematic schemes that link them to their surroundings or local history.

Creating a new maze, from conception, design and construction to the formal opening, can be a compelling experience for the owner. Lady Brunner at Greys Court, Oxfordshire, described the various craftsmen involved as her 'band of brothers' and herself chose the inscriptions on the central pillar; Mrs Veronica Tritton at Parham Park, West Sussex, relived her childhood by placing the maze where she had played on her bicycle as a girl. In some ways creating a maze is like painting a portrait,

with the age-old relationship between patron and artist developing between maze owner and designer. The maze designer may start with the owner's ideas, the history of the location, and stories, traditions and aspects of contemporary life; practical matters such as deciding dimensions, specifying materials and designing the puzzle follow later.

The modern fascination with mazes deserves explaining. A maze is the ultimate landscape artefact that one can enter, put oneself into and interact with. Experiencing a maze involves continual movement, so that one's perspective constantly changes. It is the element of fun, of probing the puzzle, of a journey of discovery, that continues to fascinate. The maze invites exploration and wonder and, like all the best games, is astonishingly simple in its concept. It also has advantages over other theme park attractions; visitors can make their own choices and progress at their own pace, and they do not have to queue to join in the fun.

19

Yet a maze can also convey imagery and symbolism, from the entertaining and frivolous to the sublime, so that the pleasure of solving the physical puzzle is heightened by discovering its secret mysteries. The fantastic Beatles' Maze (no longer existing) with its 18 tonne steel Yellow Submarine, at the 1984 Liverpool Garden Festival, and the contemplative Archbishops' Maze at Greys Court, Oxfordshire, abounding in Christian symbolism, were both entirely appropriate in their different ways.

One of the delights of Britain's mazes is their diversity. Because of the climate and the national enthusiasm for gardens, hedge mazes are particularly characteristic of Britain. The eight surviving ancient turf mazes have been joined by a remarkable variety of modern turf mazes, using paths of brick, stone or gravel instead of the traditional turf to walk on. Pavement mazes have been made both in stone and with various colours of brick. Other modern mazes make use of wood, water, mosaic, marble and stained glass. At Wookey Hole Caves in Somerset the maze walls are giant mirrors which provide tantalising reflections of colourful fountains dancing to music at its goal.

The nature of puzzlement has also developed. Turf mazes have been transformed by adding junctions and one-way rules, which make them into puzzle mazes; their size makes it difficult to work out the whole puzzle at once, and, perhaps surprisingly, children tend not to cheat in them.

An added refinement in several modern hedge mazes is a quick exit route, so that visitors do not have to wander through the maze again to get out. Sometimes this involves going over or under a bridge, as at Scone Palace in Tayside and Merritown House in Dorset. In the yew-hedge maze at Leeds Castle, Kent, the explorer reaches a high central tower, then goes underground into a decorated grotto with water cascades and spotlit statues in niches and can take a quick exit through a 90 foot (30 metre) secret tunnel running beneath the hedges.

Colour mazes are another modern innovation; they can be laid out in coloured brick paving, or, as at Flambards Theme Park in Cornwall, in interlocking plastic coloured tiles. In colour mazes the junction squares are connected by paths of different colours, and each time one reaches a node one must leave on a path of a different colour; the object, as with all mazes, is finally to reach a goal. In some colour mazes one can change to any other path colour. In others one must follow a strict colour sequence repeatedly (for example, red-brown-buff, red-brown-buff, et cetera); this is the principle involved in the brick pavement colour maze in front of the Mathematics Building at Leicester University.

Mazes are found in the most unexpected places. The public perception is sometimes simply of hedge mazes 'like the one at Hampton Court'. Turf mazes on commons and village greens come as a surprise. New puzzle mazes are found at zoos, amusement parks and in holiday areas. Outdoor pavement mazes bring vitality to courtyards and city centres, whilst indoors there are floor mazes, wall mazes in ceramic tile or mosaic, stained glass maze windows and mirror mazes.

MODERN HEDGE MAZES

Stately homes provide landscape settings for many impressive new hedge mazes, including the yew maze at Chatsworth House in Derbyshire, and the beech mazes at Scone Palace, Tayside, and Russborough House in County Wicklow, Ireland.

Hedge mazes have been created larger than ever before, with bridges and other high viewing points proving very popular with visitors. For sheer puzzlement, few compare with the giant three-dimensional maze at Longleat House in Wiltshire; it is the world's largest hedge maze and can take over an hour to solve, with its various wooden bridges and spiralling hedges creating perpetual disorientation.

On this grand scale hedge mazes provide superb opportunities for conveying imagery and symbolism. The Marlborough Maze at Blenheim Palace in Oxfordshire is the world's largest symbolic hedge maze; it portrays the panoply of victory at the battle of Blenheim and was inspired by Grinling Gibbons's decorative stone carvings on the roof of the palace. The lines of the hedges form images of trumpets, banners, cannon-

Right: *The hedge maze at Newquay Zoo, Cornwall, is in the shape of a giant dragon. Waist-high hedges make this a popular maze with children.*

Left: *The maze barriers at Bicton Park in Devon are made of upright wooden logs. The overall shape is of a giant footprint, 160 feet (49 metres) long.*

Right: *The world's largest hedge maze is at Longleat House in Wiltshire. Six bridges incorporated within the maze make this a three-dimensional puzzle.*

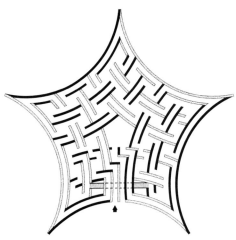

Above left: *The design of the beech-hedge maze at Russborough House in County Wicklow, Republic of Ireland, includes a diamond motif, reflecting the Beit family's early involvement in the diamond industry.*

Above right: *The beech-hedge maze at Scone Palace in Tayside is in the shape of the family's five-pointed Murray star. The rows of intersecting hedges are planted alternately in green and copper beech, thus creating a woven tartan effect.*

Below left: *The beech hedges of the Saxon Maze at The Herb Farm in Sonning Common, near Reading, are in the shape of four eighth-century Saxon sea creatures. With their culinary, medicinal and aromatic properties, herbs played an indispensable part in Saxon life.*

Below right: *The hedges of the Alice in Wonderland Maze at Merritown House, Hurn, Dorset, portray various characters from the story of Alice by Lewis Carroll.*

The hedges of the Marlborough Maze at Blenheim Palace in Oxfordshire portray cannonballs, a cannon, banners, flags and trumpets. These images were inspired by stone carvings by Grinling Gibbons on the roof of the palace.

balls and a giant cannon, and the maze incorporates high wooden bridges and brick and stone pavilions.

Sir Charles Wolseley's Britannia Maze at Wolseley Garden Park in Staffordshire portrays the image of Britannia in lines of hedges, within an outline of Britain 400 feet (122 metres) long, best appreciated from the stone tower in the centre of her shield.

The Saxon Maze at The Herb Farm in Sonning Common, near Reading, derives its hedge design from Saxon sea creatures illustrated in an eighth-century manuscript; the eyes of the creatures are planted with herbs. The maze is surrounded by an earth

rampart and approached over water. At Newquay Zoo in Cornwall a mythical beast is the labyrinth itself, since the sinuous hedges form the coils of a dragon.

The centrepiece of a new 7 acre (2.8 ha) garden at Merritown House in Dorset is a maze based on *Alice's Adventures in Wonderland*, the design of which includes outline figures of Alice, the Mad Hatter, the Dodo and other characters from the story. These are not apparent while visitors are wandering through the puzzle. They have to find their way to the centre and climb a mound, representing the White Rabbit's watch, before the figures become clear.

The Jubilee Maze at Symonds Yat West, Herefordshire, was built by the brothers Lindsay and Edward Heyes. It was planted during the Silver Jubilee year of Queen Elizabeth II in 1977. Visitors are welcomed by one of the maze owners wearing a boater and blazer.

23

The spirit of earlier ages continues to be recreated in various ways. The Jubilee Maze at Symonds Yat, Herefordshire, was inspired by the concept of the Labyrinth of Love of the late fifteenth and sixteenth centuries; it is relatively simple in design and has a temple at the centre and a raised viewing platform from which to admire the maze after solving it.

The renewed interest in historical gardens in the 1980s has led to some exciting and ambitious restoration schemes. Documentary and oral sources, combined with new archaeological techniques developed specifically to investigate abandoned gardens, have enabled accurate restorations to be made of several Victorian hedge mazes. These include mazes at Bridge End Gardens at Saffron Walden in Essex, Rhinefield House in Hampshire, Castle Bromwich Hall Gardens in West Midlands and Crystal Palace Park in south London.

MODERN TURF MAZES

Traditional turf mazes are nowadays impractical, since their turf paths cannot withstand the wear and tear of large numbers of visitors. To overcome this, several modern turf mazes have paths of hard paving, yet grass remains the dominant feature, being used as the barrier between the paths.

The Archbishop's Maze at Greys Court, Oxfordshire, dedicated by the Archbishop of Canterbury, Dr Robert Runcie, in 1981, consists of brick paths winding between wide strips of turf. It was conceived by Lady Brunner in response to a passage in the address Dr Runcie made at his enthronement in which he described a dream he had had about a maze whose pattern was clear to those who stood outside it but puzzling to those who 'fretted and fumed inside'. The maze is full of Christian symbolism, with a Latin cross and a Byzantine cross combined at its centre, to proclaim the reconciliation of East and West.

'Dolphins', one of the seven gaze mazes within the centrepiece of the Bath Festival Maze. Follow the white path by eye from tail to tail.

The design of the turf maze at Chenies Manor in Buckinghamshire was based on one shown in the background of a portrait of Edward, Lord Russell, dated 1573, which now hangs in Woburn Abbey, Bedfordshire.

The design of the stone paths of the Bath Festival Maze in the Beazer Gardens echoes the ellipses of the bridges and fan windows of Bath and incorporates a Roman key pattern.

The elegant spiralling brick maze at Parham Park in West Sussex echoes intricate Elizabethan needlework displayed within the house and is also a baffling one-way puzzle maze, in that one must keep going forwards once one has started. By contrast, railway engines provide inspiration for path mazes at the Lappa Valley Railway in Cornwall and near Newcastle upon Tyne, respectively portraying Richard Trevithick's tramroad locomotive and George Stephenson's *Rocket*.

The paths of the Bath Festival Maze, Avon, are appropriately in local Bath stone, contrasting vividly with the darker grass barriers; its centrepiece is a giant mosaic of 72,000 pieces of Italian marble, 15 feet (5 metres) in diameter, portraying the famous Gorgon's head and other aspects of Bath's Celtic and Roman past. Each of seven mosaic panels forms a 'gaze maze' which can be followed and solved by eye, and this provides a fascinating reward for reaching the centre.

PAVEMENT MAZES

The Tudor Rose Maze fills the courtyard of Kentwell Hall in Suffolk, and windows at every level look out on to the design. Made of 26,000 paving bricks in different colours, it is the world's largest brick pavement maze and can be enjoyed either as a puzzle maze or as five separate unicursal mazes. Its fifteen diamonds contain incised brick images relating to the Tudor dynasty, whilst the centre forms a giant chessboard.

The pedestrianised town centre at Worksop in Nottinghamshire has a brick pavement maze at each end, each having an heraldic theme — a Lion Rampant and a Unicorn Rampant. Using four colours of brickwork, the maze paths weave in and out of the bodies of these giant creatures before finally reaching the goal of either the lion's crown or the unicorn's horn.

Top: *The Lion Rampant Maze in Worksop town centre, Nottinghamshire. Lions appear in the heraldic devices of the Dukes of Norfolk and of Kingston, two of the five 'Dukeries' of Nottinghamshire.*

Above: *The Unicorn Rampant Maze in Worksop town centre. As in the lion design, the maze puzzle runs in and out of the body of the creature, before finally reaching the goal at its head. The darker bricks always form the barrier.*

Other pavement mazes are at the Abbotswood Shopping Centre in Yate, Gloucestershire, with a stag beetle and ant in the design, and at Edinburgh Zoo, where an orang-utan is at the centre of the Darwin hedge maze, opened in 1995.

OTHER FORMS OF MAZE

On a much smaller scale, the wall mosaic maze in Wyck Rissington church in Gloucestershire is set at a low level so that children can trace it with their fingers; it is in memory of Canon Harry Cheales, a former rector of the parish, who built a full-size maze to the same design in the rectory garden after having a vivid dream.

The maze path of the Bristol Water Maze in Victoria Park, Bristol, is a water channel running between barriers of brick and is primarily to be looked at rather than walked along; its design comes from the medieval Christian roof-boss maze in St Mary Redcliffe church nearby.

At Legoland, near Windsor, Berkshire, a hedge maze opened in 1996 incorporates a walk-through parting waterfall and fountain gates to block or open the path.

The Beatles' Maze at the 1984 Liverpool International Garden Festival also incorporated water, but here as the barrier between raised brick paths; the whole concept was of a psychedelic garden, with stepping stones in the shape of musical notes, and a ring of apple trees planted around it. A million people walked through it during the six months of the festival.

The Royal National Institute for the Blind commissioned a maze for teaching its students. It opened in 1993 and has different types of vertical barrier and path surfaces.

Flat portable mazes of coloured plastic tiles are popular in leisure parks, schools and even on cruise ships.

The diversity of Britain's mazes is unparalleled anywhere in the world and continues to develop with new and delightful creations. Let us hope that mazes will entertain and fascinate for many generations to come.

The labyrinthine water channel of the Bristol Water Maze derives its design from a roof boss in St Mary Redcliffe church, on which its axis is aligned.

FURTHER READING AND ORGANISATIONS

BOOKS

Fisher, Adrian, and Gerster, George. *The Art of the Maze*. Weidenfeld & Nicolson, 1990. The modern definitive work on mazes worldwide, with over a hundred colour illustrations.

Fisher, Adrian. *Your Land Is His Canvas*. Adrian Fisher Maze Design, 1997. Booklet illustrating Adrian Fisher's work as a maze designer.

Kraft, John. *The Goddess in the Labyrinth*. Abo Akademi, 1985.

Matthews, W.H. *Mazes and Labyrinths – Their History and Development*. 1922; reprinted by Dover, New York, 1970. Definitive work on mazes, though inevitably deficient on the twentieth century.

Pennick, Nigel. *Mazes and Labyrinths*. Robert Hale, 1990. Mazes and labyrinths in their historical context.

ORGANISATIONS

Caerdroia, 53 Thundersley Grove, Thundersley, Benfleet, Essex SS7 3EB. Telephone: 01268 751915. Its magazine, *Caerdroia*, is edited by Jeff Saward: many issues since 1980.

Adrian Fisher Maze Design, 5 Victoria Grove, Portsmouth, Hampshire PO5 1NE. Telephone: 01705 355500.

MAZES TO VISIT

This is a list of mazes and labyrinths of all kinds that are accessible to the public in the United Kingdom and the Republic of Ireland. However, new mazes are being created every year and occasionally an existing maze ceases to be open to the public. Many are at historic houses, gardens or other tourist attractions and intending visitors are advised to find out the opening times before making a special journey. The National Grid reference (NGR) is given for certain hard-to-find sites.

ENGLAND

BERKSHIRE

The Herb Farm, Sonning Common, near Reading, Berkshire RG4 9NJ. Telephone: 01734 724220. The Saxon Maze (hedge maze).

Legoland, near Windsor. Telephone: 01990 040404. Tudor hedge maze with parting waterfall, Celtic maze and nautical maze.

BRISTOL

Bristol: Exploratory Science Centre, Bristol Old Station, Temple Meads, Bristol BS1 6QU. 'Circle 12' colour maze.

Bristol: St Mary Redcliffe church. Roof-boss maze.

Bristol: Victoria Park. Water maze.

BUCKINGHAMSHIRE

Chenies Manor House, Chenies, near Rickmansworth WD3 6ER. Telephone: 01494 762888. Gravel paths in grass maze. Also Chenies Hedge Maze, winner of *Sunday Times* maze design competition, created during 1991.

Willen Lake, Milton Keynes. Gravel paths in grass maze.

CAMBRIDGESHIRE

Bourn, near Cambridge: church of St Helen and St Mary. Pavement maze.

Ely Cathedral. Pavement maze.

Hilton, near Huntingdon. The Common (NGR TL 293663). Turf maze.

CHESHIRE

Parkfield, Warrington. Gravel paths in grass maze.

Tatton Park, Knutsford WA16 6QB. National Trust. Telephone: 01565 654822. Hedge maze.

CORNWALL

Flambards Theme Park, Culdrose Manor, Helston TR13 0GA. Telephone: 01326 574549. Children's colour maze.

Glendurgan Garden, Mawnan Smith, near Falmouth TR11 5JZ. National Trust. Telephone: 01326 250906. Hedge maze.

Holywell Bay Leisure Park, near Newquay. Telephone: 01637 830095. Wooden fencing maze with bridges, parting waterfall and fountain gates.

Lappa Valley Steam Railway and Leisure Park, St Newlyn East, Newquay TR8 5HZ. Telephone: 01872 510317. Brick paths in grass maze.

Newquay Zoo, Newquay. Telephone: 01637 873342. Hedge maze.

Rocky Valley, near Tintagel. Rock carvings.

St Agnes, Scilly Isles: NGR SV 876078, 878078. Stone labyrinths.

St Martin's, Scilly Isles: NGR SV 923170. Stone labyrinths.

CUMBRIA

Holker Hall and Gardens, Cark-in-Cartmel LA11 7PL. Telephone: 01539 558328. Children's colour mazes.

DERBYSHIRE

Chatsworth House, near Bakewell DE4 1PP. Telephone: 01246 582204. Hedge maze.

Heights of Abraham Country Park, Matlock Bath. Children's colour maze.

DEVON

Bicton Park, East Budleigh, Budleigh Salterton EX9 7DP. Telephone: 01395 568465. Wooden-walled maze.

South Devon Railway, Buckfastleigh TQ11 0DZ. Telephone: 01364 642338. Hedge maze.

DORSET

Merritown House, Hurn, Christchurch. Telephone: 01202 483004. Alice in Wonderland Maze (hedge maze).

EAST YORKSHIRE

Burton Agnes Hall, Burton Agnes, Driffield. Telephone: 01262 490324. Hedge maze.

Hull: King Edward Street. Brick pavement maze.

ESSEX

Bridge End Gardens, Saffron Walden. Telephone (tourist information centre): 01799 510444. Hedge maze.

Hadstock, near Saffron Walden. St Botolph's churchyard. Maze on gravestone of Michael Ayrton.

Mistley Place Park, Manningtree CO11 1ER. Telephone: 01206 396483. Hedge maze.

Saffron Walden: The Common (NGR TL 543385). Turf maze.

GLOUCESTERSHIRE

Abbotswood Shopping Centre, Yate. Four circular coloured brick pavement mazes with a stag beetle and an ant in the brickwork; by Adrian Fisher, 1994.

The gravestone of the sculptor Michael Ayrton in Hadstock churchyard, Essex, includes an 18 inch (457 mm) wide bronze replica of the full-size brick labyrinth he built at Arkville, New York state, USA.

The wall mosaic maze in Wyck Rissington church in Gloucestershire is based on the fifteen Mysteries of the Gospels; these are indicated in Roman numerals and can be traced in sequence to the goal without once crossing over one's path.

Wyck Rissington, near Stow-on-the-Wold: St Lawrence's church. Maze of the Mysteries of the Gospels (wall mosaic).

HAMPSHIRE
Breamore Countryside Museum, Breamore House, Breamore, Fordingbridge, Hampshire SP6 2DF. Telephone: 01725 512468. Great British Maze (brick paths in grass maze).
Breamore Down: Miz-maze (NGR SU 142203). Turf maze.
Itchen Stoke, near Winchester: St Mary's church. Pavement maze beneath altar.
Paultons Park, Ower, near Romsey SO51 6AL. Telephone: 01703 814442.
Rhinefield House Hotel, near Brockenhurst. Hedge maze.
St Catherine's Hill, near Winchester: Miz-maze. Turf maze.
Southampton: Mayflower Park. Concrete-walled maze.

HEREFORDSHIRE
Hereford Cathedral. Mappa Mundi – maze representing Crete.
Jubilee Maze, Symonds Yat West, Ross-on-Wye HR9 6BY. Telephone: 01600 890360. Hedge maze and museum of mazes.

HERTFORDSHIRE
Hatfield House, Hatfield AL9 5NF. Telephone: 01707 262823. Low box maze (may be viewed but not walked in).
Tring: zebra head brick maze by parish church.

ISLE OF WIGHT
Blackgang Chine, near Ventnor PO38 2HN. Telephone: 01983 730330. Hedge maze.

KENT
Hever Castle, Hever, Edenbridge TN8 7NG. Telephone: 01732 865224. Hedge maze.
Leeds Castle, Maidstone ME17 1PL. Telephone: 01622 765400. Hedge maze and grotto.

LANCASHIRE
Blackpool Pleasure Beach, Blackpool. Telephone: 01253 341033. Hedge maze.
Leighton Hall, Yealand Conyers, Carnforth LA5 9ST. Telephone: 01524 734474. The Caterpillar Maze (gravel paths in grass maze).
Worden Park, Leyland. Hedge maze.

LEICESTERSHIRE
Leicester University, Leicester. 'Mathematica' (brick pavement colour maze in front of Mathematics Building).

LINCOLNSHIRE
Alkborough, near Scunthorpe: church of St John the Baptist. Stained glass window maze; stone pavement maze in porch.
Alkborough, near Scunthorpe: Julian's Bower (NGR SE 880218). Turf maze.
Doddington Hall, Doddington, Lincoln. Telephone: 01522 694308. Gravel paths in grass maze.
Springfields Gardens, Spalding PE12 6ET. Telephone: 01775 724843. Hedge maze.

LONDON
Capel Manor, Bullsmoor Lane, Enfield, Middlesex EN1 4RQ. Telephone: 0181-366 4442. Italianate maze (hedge maze).
Crystal Palace Park, London SE19. Crystal Palace Maze (hedge maze).
Hampton Court Palace, East Molesey, Surrey KT8 9AH. Telephone: 0181-781 9787. Hedge maze.
Warren Street Playground, Whitfield Street, London W1. Pavement maze.
Warren Street Underground Station, London W1. Wall mazes of ceramic tiles.

NORTH YORKSHIRE
Dalby, near Malton: City of Troy (NGR SE 626719). Turf maze.
Scarborough: Victoria Park. Hedge maze.

NOTTINGHAMSHIRE
Worksop: town centre precinct. Lion Rampant and Unicorn Rampant pavement mazes.

OXFORDSHIRE
Blenheim Palace, Woodstock OX7 1PX. Telephone: 01993 811325. Marlborough Maze (hedge maze).
Greys Court, Rotherfield Greys, Henley-on-Thames. National Trust. Telephone: 01491 628529. Archbishop's Maze (brick path in grass).

RUTLAND
Wing, near Oakham: The Common (NGR SK 895028). Turf maze.

SHROPSHIRE
Burford House Gardens, Burford, near Tenbury Wells WR15 8HQ. Telephone: 01584 810777. Hedge maze.
Telford: Telford Town Park. Wonderland Maze (hedge maze).

SOMERSET
Bath: Beazer Gardens, near Pulteney Bridge. Bath Festival Maze (stone path in grass maze).
Batheaston, near Bath: church. Pavement maze.
Wookey Hole Caves, Wookey Hole, Wells BA5 1BB. Telephone: 01749 672243. Magical Mirror Maze.

SUFFOLK
Kentwell Hall, Long Melford CO10 9BA. Telephone: 01787 310207. Tudor Rose Maze (pavement maze).
Somerleyton Hall, Somerleyton, Lowestoft NR32 5QQ. Telephone: 01502 730224. Hedge maze.

SURREY
Watts Memorial Chapel, Compton, near Guildford GU3 1DQ. Telephone: 01483 810235. Corbels and altar decoration, incorporating labyrinths.

TYNE AND WEAR
Saltwell Park, Gateshead. Hedge maze (may be viewed from above but not walked in).
Springfield Park, Forest Hall, near Newcastle upon Tyne. Rocket Maze (gravel paths in turf maze).

WARWICKSHIRE
Ragley Hall, near Alcester B49 5NJ. Telephone: 01789 762090. Concrete-walled maze.

WEST MIDLANDS
Castle Bromwich Hall Gardens, Chester Road, Castle Bromwich, West Midlands B36 9BT. Telephone: 0121-749 4100. Hedge maze.

WEST SUSSEX
County Mall, Crawley. Two terrazzo paving mazes.
Parham House and Gardens, near Pulborough RH20 4HS. Telephone: 01903 744888. Veronica's Maze (brick paths in grass maze).

WEST YORKSHIRE
Eureka Children's Museum, Halifax HX1 2NE. Telephone: 01422 330069. Children's colour mazes.
Temple Newsam House, near Leeds LS15 0AE. Telephone: 0113-264 7321. Pavement maze.

WILTSHIRE
Longleat House, near Warminster. Telephone: 01985 844400. Hedge mazes.

SCOTLAND
BORDERS
Traquair House, Innerleithen EH44 6PW. Telephone: 01896 830323. Hedge maze.

GRAMPIAN
Hazlehead Park, Aberdeen. Hedge maze.

HIGHLAND
Blervie House, Nairn. Ziggurat (hedge) maze.
Landmark Centre, Carrbridge, Inverness-shire. Telephone: 01479 841613. Raised wooden paths in
  woodland.
Strathpeffer, near Dingwall, Ross and Cromarty. Touchstone Maze.

LOTHIAN
Edinburgh Zoo, Edinburgh. Telephone: 0131-334 9171. The Darwin Maze: a hedge maze around two
  pavement mazes.

STRATHCLYDE
Finlaystone House and Gardens, Langbank PA14 6TJ. Telephone: 01475 540285. Granite paths in
  grass maze.
Irvine: Ayrshire Beach Park. Concrete paths in grass maze.
Irvine, Ayrshire: New Town Centre. Stained glass window maze.

TAYSIDE
Scone Palace, near Perth PH2 6BD. Telephone: 01738 552300. Murray Maze (hedge maze).

WALES
GLAMORGAN
Margam Country Park, Port Talbot. Telephone: 01639 881635. Hedge maze.
Rose Hill Quarry, near Swansea: NGR SS 644935. Rose Hill Quarry Labyrinth (gravel paths in grass
  maze).
Techniquest Science Centre, Cardiff. 'Square 12' colour maze, by Adrian Fisher, 1992.
Three Cliffs Bay, Pennard, Gower: NGR SS 539882. Stone labyrinth.

GWENT
Roman Legionary Museum, High Street, Caerleon NP6 1AE. Telephone: 01633 423134. Roman
  mosaic labyrinth.

POWYS
Llangoed Hall, Llyswen, Brecon. Telephone: 01874 754525. Hedge maze.
National Centre for Alternative Technology, Machynlleth SY20 9AZ. Telephone: 01654 702400.
  Environmental Maze (hedge maze).

NORTHERN IRELAND
Carnfunock Amenity Park, County Antrim.

REPUBLIC OF IRELAND
Burt, County Donegal: St Regnus church.
Dunbrody Abbey, County Wexford. Hedge maze.
National Museum of Ireland, Kildare Street, Dublin 2. Telephone: (01) 677 7444. The Hollywood Stone.
Rathmore, County Meath: Rathmore Maze, Rathmore church.
Russborough House, Blessington, County Wicklow. Telephone: 045 65239. Hedge maze.